HIDDEN HISTORY FOR KIDS

Awesome Activists

Claudette Colvin

Making a Move for Justice

Before Rosa Parks, fifteen-year-old **Claudette Colvin** stayed in her bus seat instead of giving it to a White passenger. Because of this, she was arrested. **Claudette Colvin** showed that standing up for what's right can sometimes mean staying in your seat.

Rabbi Lynn Gottlieb

Standing up for Peace

Rabbi Lynn Gottlieb believes in making the world a kinder and more peaceful place. She speaks up for people who are treated unfairly and works to bring different communities together. **Rabbi Gottlieb** shows that faith and fairness go hand in hand.

Alice Wong

Fighting for Disability Rights

Alice Wong believes that everyone deserves to be included. She created a group to help disabled people share their stories and speak up for their rights. **Alice Wong** shows that every voice matters, no matter how it is heard.

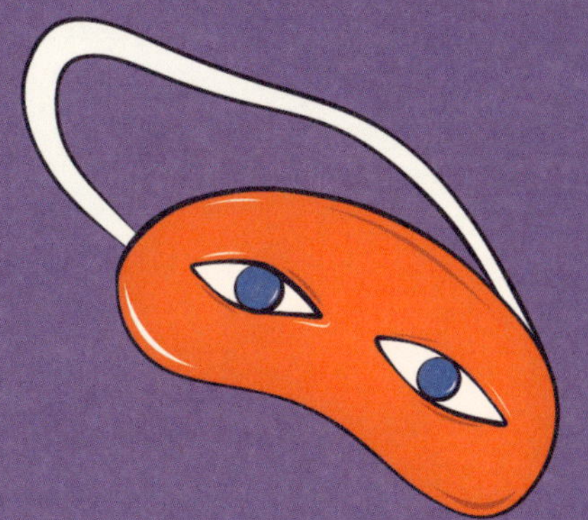

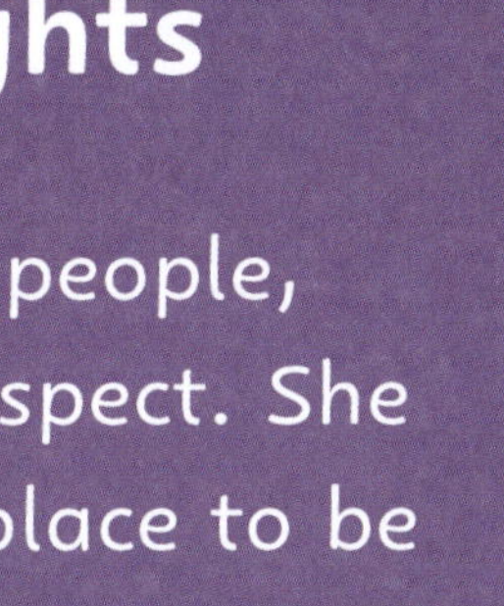

Sylvia Rivera

Standing Proud for LGBTQ+ Rights

Sylvia Rivera worked hard to make sure LGBTQ+ people, especially those without homes, had support and respect. She helped start organizations that gave people a safe place to be themselves. **Sylvia Rivera** showed that fighting for fairness means making sure no one is left out.

Harvey Milk

Breaking Barriers in Government

In 1977, **Harvey Milk** was the first openly gay man elected to office in California. He wanted to make the world a safer and kinder place for LGBTQ+ people. **Harvey Milk** showed that change happens when leaders stand up for their communities.

To the
President
Obama
Little Miss

Mari Copeny
"Little Miss Flint"

Speaking Up for Clean Water

When **Mari Copeny** was only eight years old, she wrote a letter to President Obama because the water in her town was dirty and not safe to drink. People all over heard her message, and she became a leader in the fight for clean water. **Mari Copeny** showed that one person's voice can lead to big changes.

Rocking for Refugees

Eugene Hütz is a musician who uses his songs to tell the world about refugees—people who have to leave their homes because of war or danger. He celebrates his Romani roots and helps people stay proud of where they come from. **Eugene Hütz** shows that music can bring people together and tell important stories.

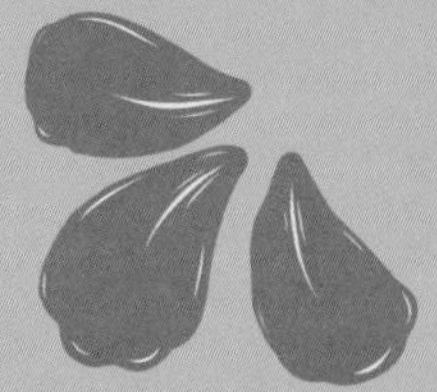

The Grimké Sisters

Sisters for Freedom and Equality

Sarah and **Angelina Grimké** grew up in a time when people didn't want women to speak up, but they didn't let that stop them. They spoke out against slavery and worked for equal rights for all. The **Grimké Sisters** showed that being brave means using your voice, even when people don't want to listen.

Cesar Chavez

Fighting for Fairness at Work

Cesar Chavez helped farm workers get better pay and safe places to work. He brought them together so their voices could be heard. **Cesar Chavez** showed that people can make big changes when they stand together for what's right.

Madonna Thunder Hawk

A Protector of Native Rights

Madonna Thunder Hawk is a Lakota leader who has spent her whole life fighting for Indigenous rights. She works to protect Native lands, water, and traditions. **Madonna Thunder Hawk** shows that protecting the earth and its people is a fight worth standing up for.

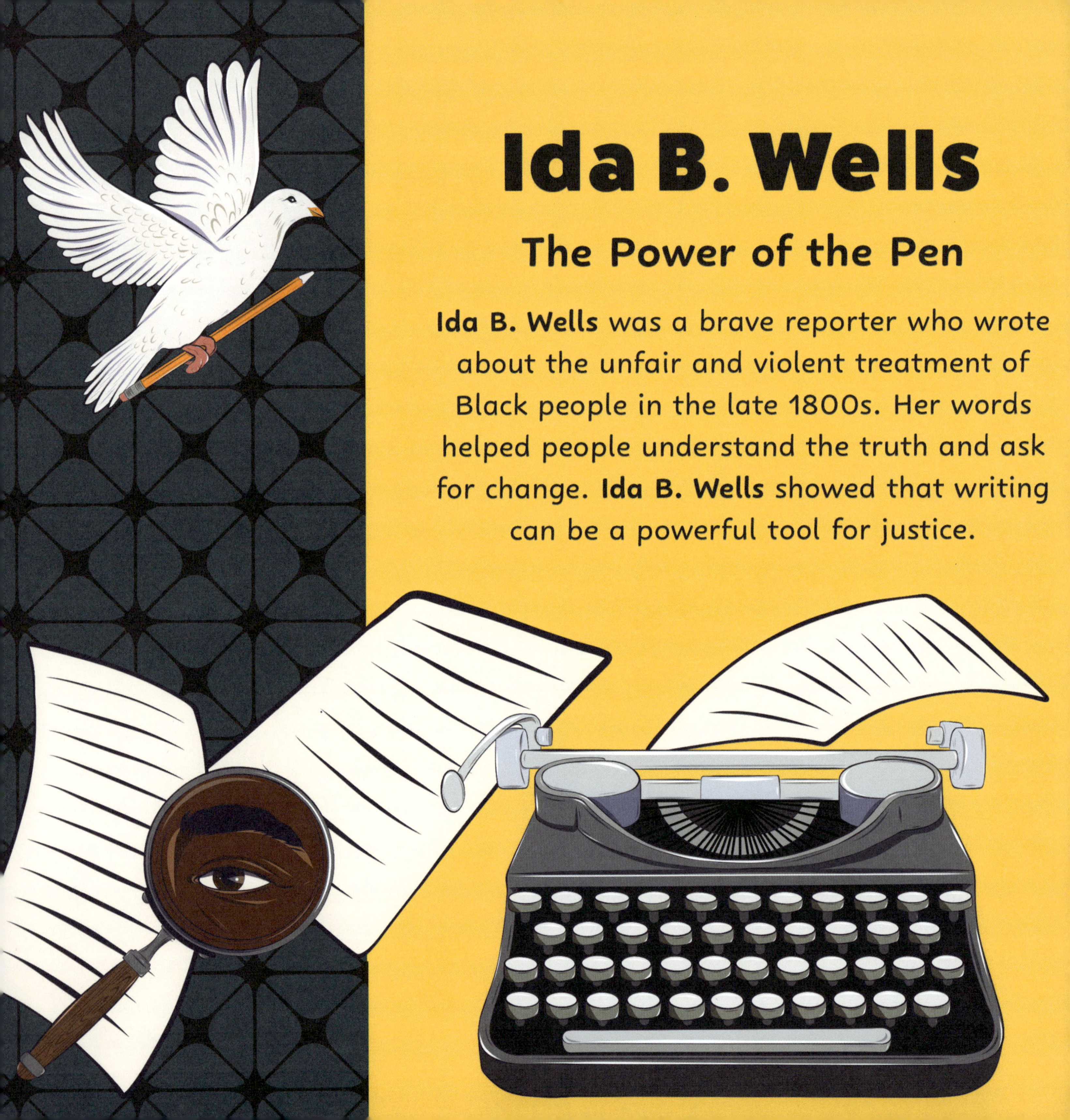

Ida B. Wells

The Power of the Pen

Ida B. Wells was a brave reporter who wrote about the unfair and violent treatment of Black people in the late 1800s. Her words helped people understand the truth and ask for change. **Ida B. Wells** showed that writing can be a powerful tool for justice.

Ilhan Abdullahi Omar

Breaking Barriers in Politics

Ilhan Omar became one of the first Muslim women in the U.S. Congress. As a former refugee, she speaks up for people who are often ignored and works to make sure everyone has a fair chance in life. **Ilhan Abdullahi Omar** shows that leaders can come from all backgrounds and beliefs.

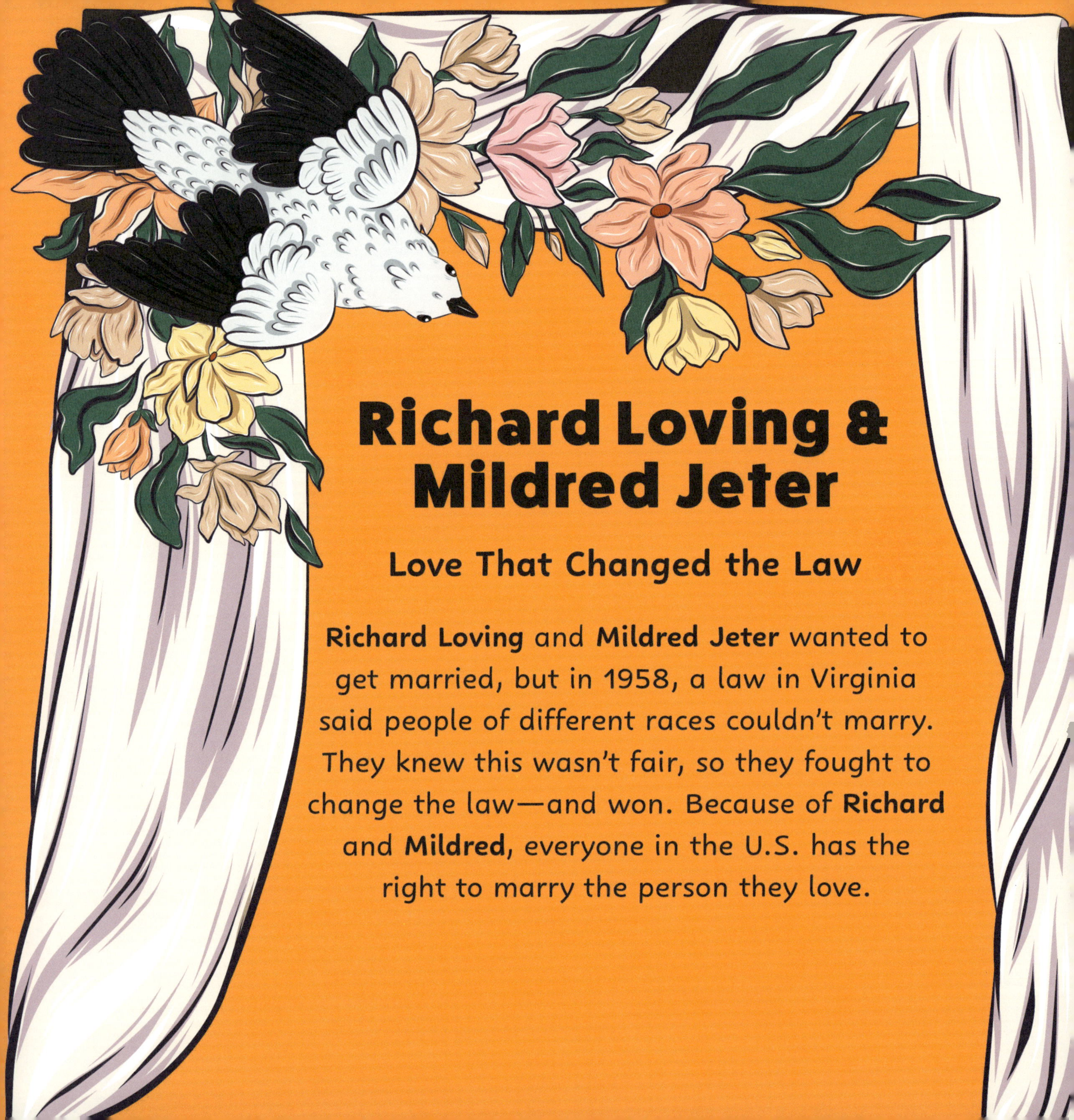

Richard Loving & Mildred Jeter

Love That Changed the Law

Richard Loving and **Mildred Jeter** wanted to get married, but in 1958, a law in Virginia said people of different races couldn't marry. They knew this wasn't fair, so they fought to change the law—and won. Because of **Richard** and **Mildred**, everyone in the U.S. has the right to marry the person they love.

Yuri Kochiyama

Fighting for Justice for All

Yuri Kochiyama was sent to an internment camp as a child because of her Japanese heritage. Instead of staying silent, she spent her life standing up for the rights of all people facing injustice. **Yuri Kochiyama** shows that we can turn pain into power by fighting for what's right.

Tarana Burke

Sharing Stories to Empower Survivors

Tarana Burke started the **#MeToo** movement to help people, especially women, share their experiences with abuse. Her idea spread around the world and got people talking about safety and respect. **Tarana Burke** showed that speaking up can help others do the same.

#MeToo
#MeToo
#MeToo
#MeToo
#MeToo
#MeToo
#MeToo

Claudette Colvin

Before Rosa Parks became famous for refusing to give up her bus seat, **Claudette Colvin** made history by doing the same thing at just 15 years old. On March 2, 1955, Claudette was arrested for not giving up her seat to a White passenger on a bus in Alabama. Civil rights leaders first thought her case might end bus segregation, but it didn't move forward. Later, Rosa Parks' protest became the spark that started the Montgomery Bus Boycott, which was a huge step in the fight for civil rights in the United States.

Rabbi Lynn Gottlieb

Rabbi Lynn Gottlieb is a peace activist, writer, and one of the first women to become a rabbi in the U.S. She has spent her life working for peace and justice. She co-founded the Muslim-Jewish Arts Collective to bring people from different faiths together through art. She is also active in supporting Palestinian rights, nuclear disarmament, and nonviolent protests. Rabbi Gottlieb travels around the world to speak out for people who are being treated unfairly and works hard to build understanding between different groups of people.

Alice Wong

Alice Wong is a disability rights activist and the founder of the Disability Visibility Project, which helps disabled people share their stories. She has worked with leaders to create better policies for people with disabilities and speaks out against ableism. Wong uses a ventilator because of a neuromuscular disability but is a strong leader in digital activism. She shows how people can make big changes even if they can't always be there in person. Through her writing and speaking, Wong inspires others to fight for fairness and equal access.

Sylvia Rivera

Sylvia Rivera was a transgender activist who co-founded STAR (Street Transvestite Action Revolutionaries) with Marsha P. Johnson. She spent her life helping homeless LGBTQ+ youth and standing up for transgender rights. Sylvia was a leader during the Stonewall uprising in 1969, where she bravely stood up to the police. Even when some LGBTQ+ groups left out trans people and people of color, Sylvia kept fighting to make sure no one was forgotten. Her work helped start many of the protections LGBTQ+ people have today, and she is remembered as a true fighter.

Harvey Milk

Harvey Milk was a leader for LGBTQ+ rights and became the first openly gay person elected to public office in California in 1977. He worked hard to make sure LGBTQ+ people were treated equally and supported laws to protect them from unfair treatment. Harvey believed it was important for people to be proud of who they are. As a community organizer and public servant, he brought people together and helped push for change. His courage and leadership inspired many others to stand up for LGBTQ+ rights across the country.

Mari Copeny

Mari Copeny, known as "Little Miss Flint," became a national voice for clean water when she was only 8 years old. She wrote a letter to President Obama about the water crisis in Flint, Michigan and got national attention. Mari has kept speaking out to help communities facing unsafe drinking water. She also helped create a special water filter that helps families all over the country. Mari continues to inspire people with her hard work and shows that kids can be powerful leaders in making change.

Eugene Hütz

Eugene Hütz is the lead singer of the band Gogol Bordello, which mixes punk rock with Romani and Eastern European music. Born in Ukraine, Eugene came to the United States as a refugee. His music tells stories about being an immigrant and a refugee, and he speaks out for immigrant rights. His band is known for exciting live shows that bring people of different cultures together. Through his music and activism, Eugene works to make sure refugees and immigrants are treated with respect and kindness.

The Grimké Sisters

Sarah and Angelina Grimké were sisters born into a rich Southern family that enslaved Black people, but they became strong abolitionists. They spoke out against slavery and fought for women's rights. One of their most famous writings, "Appeal to the Christian Women of the South," asked women to stand up against slavery. The Grimké sisters gave speeches and wrote books that inspired others to join the fight for freedom and equality. They showed great courage by turning against the unfair system they were born into.

Cesar Chavez

Cesar Chavez was a leader who worked to improve life for farm workers in the United States. He believed in peaceful protests and went on hunger strikes to show his commitment. In 1968 and 1972, he fasted to remind workers to stay peaceful and strong. He also protested against pesticides that harmed farm workers. Cesar's leadership helped farm workers win better pay and safer working conditions. Even late in his life, he kept fighting for fairness. His motto, "*Sí, se puede!*" ("*Yes, we can!*"), is still used today.

Madonna Thunder Hawk

Madonna Thunder Hawk is a Lakota activist and a leader in the American Indian Movement. She has spent her life fighting for Native land and water rights. She co-founded Women of All Red Nations and continues to mentor young Indigenous activists. She helped lead the 1973 protest at Wounded Knee and later played a big role in the Standing Rock protests against a dangerous oil pipeline. Madonna works to protect Native culture and the environment, showing people how to stand up for their rights and protect their communities.

Ida B. Wells

Ida B. Wells was a brave leader in the fight for civil rights. In 1883, she was thrown off a train for refusing to leave the first-class car because she was Black. She wrote articles about this and other injustices to raise awareness. Ida was also famous for her anti-lynching work, where she told the truth about violence against Black people. In 1909, she helped start the NAACP. Through her writing and speeches, Ida fought for justice and equal rights for Black Americans.

Ilhan Abdullahi Omar

Ilhan Abdullahi Omar made history in 2018 as one of the first Muslim women elected to the U.S. Congress. Born in Somalia, she came to the United States as a refugee. In Congress, she works to support immigrants, raise the minimum wage, and fight racism. She also speaks out for refugees around the world and pushes for peaceful solutions to conflicts. Ilhan is known for standing up for fairness and speaking out even when it is difficult. She inspires people to stay strong and work for justice.

Richard Loving and Mildred Jeter

In 1958, **Richard Loving** and **Mildred Jeter** got married in Washington, DC, even though Virginia's laws banned interracial marriage. They were arrested and had to leave their home state, but they didn't give up. With help from the ACLU, they fought their case all the way to the Supreme Court. In 1967, the Court said the law was unfair, ending bans on interracial marriage across the country. Nearly fifty years later, on June 26, 2015, same-sex marriage became legal in all 50 states. Richard and Mildred's bravery is honored every year on Loving Day, which celebrates the right to marry the person you love.

Yuri Kochiyama

Yuri Kochiyama was an activist who spent her life fighting for racial justice. During World War II, her family was forced into a Japanese internment camp. Later, she worked with Malcolm X and became a strong supporter of the Black Power movement. Yuri also fought for reparations for Japanese Americans and spoke out for many different oppressed groups. She believed that people from all backgrounds should work together for justice. Her work helped build connections between communities and inspired others to keep fighting for equality.

Tarana Burke

Tarana Burke started the #MeToo movement to help survivors of sexual abuse speak out and support each other. The idea came after she talked with a young girl who had been hurt, and Tarana wanted people to know they were not alone. She also started Just Be Inc. to help young women of color. The #MeToo movement became a global call for justice, shining a light on abuse and pushing for change. Tarana's work has made it safer for people to tell their stories and demand respect.

Now Let's Talk: How Can *YOU* Make a Difference?

After reading about these inspiring activists, ask the young person with you:
"What's something you care about that you'd like to change or improve in your school, neighborhood, or even the world?"

Talk about simple ways people can help—like standing up for a friend, caring for nature, or sharing ideas to make things fairer. You might ask:
"What's one small thing you could do today to make a difference?"

About the Creators

Illustrator

Anna Rabko loves running alongside horses just to see who has longer legs and hair. Anna measures time and distance with coffee.

Researcher/Writer

Rebekah Borucki enjoys making tiny ceramic opossums, collecting more books than she can read, and visiting her children's classrooms as the Mystery Reader (shhh, it's a secret!). She lives in New Jersey with her family of two- and four-legged misfits.